SOFT ANIMALS
by HOLLY ROBINSON

soft animals was first performed on 6 February 2019 at Soho Theatre, London.

SOFT ANIMALS
by HOLLY ROBINSON

CAST

SARAH	Ellie Piercy
FRANKIE	Bianca Stephens

CREATIVES

Director	Lakesha Arie-Angelo
Designer	Anna Reid
Lighting Designer	Ali Hunter
Sound Designer	Anna Clock
Stage Manager	Kate Bachtler
Production Manager	Jack Greenyer
Producer	David Luff
Assistant Producer	Holly De Angelis
Dramaturg	Adam Brace

This production is kindly supported by Cockayne – Grants for the Arts and The London Community Foundation, and Angela Hyde-Courtney.

CAST

ELLIE PIERCY | SARAH
Ellie trained at RADA. Other theatre includes: *Sideways* (St James Theatre); *Eventide* (Arcola Theatre); *Much Ado About Nothing* (Royal Exchange Theatre, Manchester); *The Widowing of Mrs Holroyd* (Orange Tree Theatre, Richmond); *Heresy of Love, Blue Stockings, Liberty, As You Like It, All's Well That Ends Well, Merry Wives of Windsor, Romeo and Juliet* (Shakespeare's Globe); *How to Beat a Giant* (Unicorn Theatre); *Plunder* (Watermill Theatre) and *Touch of the Sun* (Salisbury Playhouse). TV and film credits include: *Black Mirror: Bandersnatch* (Netflix); *McMafia, The World of Impressionists, Doctors* (BBC); and *Brothers of War* (MCN Productions). Radio includes: *Home Front* (BBC) and *The Submarine Hunter* (Somethin' Else Productions/ BBC).

BIANCA STEPHENS | FRANKIE
Bianca trained at Royal Welsh College of Music and Drama. Theatre includes: *The Burning Tower* (S.P.I.D. Theatre/Bush Theatre); *Dames* (Pleasance Theatre); *A Midsummer Night's Dream, Julius Caesar* (Storyhouse); *E15* (Lung Theatre); *The Great Austerity Debate* (Menagerie Theatre); and *Always Orange* (Royal Shakespeare Company). Radio includes: *The Confessions of Dorian* Gray (Big Finish).

CREATIVES

HOLLY ROBINSON | WRITER

Holly is a playwright, casting assistant and nanny. She was born in Birmingham and found her love of theatre at Warwickshire's Playbox Theatre. She moved to London to pursue a degree in English Literature. *soft animals* is her first play and was longlisted for the Bruntwood Prize and shortlisted for the Tony Craze Award.

LAKESHA ARIE-ANGELO | DIRECTOR

Lakesha is Soho Theatre's Resident Director. Work as a director includes: *The Hoes* (Hampstead Theatre); *Alive Day* (Bunker Theatre for Pint Sized Plays); *AS:NT* (Theatre503, as part of Rapid Write); and *Prodigal* (Bush Theatre for 'Artistic Directors of the Future Black Lives: Black Words'). Work as Assistant Director at Soho includes: *The One, Touch, Blueberry Toast* and *Roller Diner* (2017 West End Wilma Award for Best Comedy). Work as a playwright includes *Graveyard Gang* for Tamasha Theatre's associate company Purple Moon Drama (Rich Mix/ Poplar Union/community tour). Lakesha's previous work as Resident Assistant Director at the Finborough includes: *P'Yongyang, Treasure* and *Vibrant 2015 Festival of Finborough Playwrights*. During the residency at the Finborough, Lakesha was awarded the Richard Carne Trust sponsorship.

ANNA REID | SET AND COSTUME DESIGNER

Anna is a set and costume designer based in London and a graduate of Wimbledon College of Art. Design credits include: *Paradise* and *The Hoes* (Hampstead Theatre); *Twelfth Night, The Sweet Science of Bruising, Collective Rage, Dear Brutus, The Cardinal* and *School Play* (Southwark Playhouse); *Dust* and *Rasheeda Speaking* (Trafalgar Studios), *Drip Feed, Fury* and *Brute* (Soho Theatre); *Schism* (Park Theatre); *Grotty* (Bunker Theatre); *Tiny Dynamite* (Old Red Lion Theatre); *Rattle Snake* (Live Theatre Newcastle/York Theatre Royal/Soho Theatre); *The Kitchen Sink* and *Jumpers for Goalposts* (Oldham Coliseum); *Sex Worker's Opera* (set only, national tour and Ovalhouse); *I'm Gonna Pray for You So Hard* (Finborough Theatre); *For Those Who Cry When They Hear the Foxes Scream* (Tristan Bates Theatre); *Dottir* (The Courtyard); *Dry Land* (Jermyn Street Theatre); *Arthur's World* (Bush Theatre); *Hippolytus* (V&A Museum) and *Hamlet* (Riverside Studios). www.annareiddesign.com

ALI HUNTER | LIGHTING DESIGNER

Ali lights for theatre, dance and opera and her recent credits include: *Don't Forget the Birds* and *Rattle Snake* (both Open Clasp); *Clear White Light* (Live Theatre Newcastle); *13.60* (Barking Broadway); *The War on Terry* (Landor Space); *The Boatswain's Mate* (Arcola Theatre); *The Play About My Dad* and *Woman Before a Glass* (Jermyn Street Theatre); *The Biograph Girl* and *Gracie* (Finborough Theatre); *Isaac Came Home from the Mountain* (Theatre503); *Tune-D In* (The Place); *The Acid Test* (Cockpit Theatre); *Doodle* (Waterloo East Theatre); *Tenderly* (New Wimbledon Studio); *Katzenmusik* (Royal Court Theatre); and *Foreign Body* (Women of the World and VAULT Festival). Ali is the Young Associate Lighting Designer for Matthew Bourne's *Romeo and Juliet*.

ANNA CLOCK | SOUND DESIGNER

Anna is a composer, sound designer and cellist working across theatre, film and installation. Recent projects include: *Pomona* and *Punk Rock* (New Diorama); *Bury the Dead* (Finborough Theatre); *Fabric* (Soho Theatre/community spaces tour); *Katie Johnstone, In The Night Time* and *[BLANK]* (Orange Tree Theatre, Richmond); *Overexposed* (V&A Museum); *UNCENSORED* (Royal Haymarket Theatre); *Songlines* (Edinburgh Fringe/HighTide Festival/regional tour); *Finding Fassbender* (VAULT Festival/ Edinburgh Fringe/HighTide Festival); *Forgotten Women* podcast series (Peer Productions); *Blizzard* (CentrE17; Barbican Labs); *Spun* (Arcola Theatre); *Maria* (Omnibus Theatre, CPT); *The Show* (Slade School of Fine Art). In 2018 Anna was artist in residence at SPINE Festival Borough of Harrow and Sirius Arts Centre, and holds an MA in Advanced Theatre Practice from Central School of Speech and Drama. www.annaclock.com

ADAM BRACE | ASSOCIATE DRAMATURG

Adam is Associate Dramaturg at Soho Theatre working across theatre and comedy. Recently he developed and directed Jessie Cave's hit show *Sunrise*, as well as six other comedy shows all of which transferred to Soho – including two Best Show Award nominations. As dramaturg he has worked on Vicky Jones's plays at Soho and all of Sh!t Theatre's work, including *Dollywould* and the multi-award-winning *Letters to Windsor House*. As a writer he has had plays produced by the Almeida Theatre and the National Theatre. His first screenplay won Best Short Film at Sundance London and was nominated for the same award at Sundance USA.

NADINE RENNIE CDG | CASTING DIRECTOR

Nadine has been Casting Director at Soho Theatre for over fiteen years working on new plays by writers including: Dennis Kelly, Vicky Jones, Phoebe Waller-Bridge, Roy Williams, Philip Ridley, Shelagh Stevenson, D. C. Moore, Alecky Blythe and Oladipo Agboluaje. Directors she has worked during this time include Rufus Norris, Tamara Harvey, Indhu Rubasingham, Michael Buffong, Paulette Randall, Tim Crouch, Natalie Ibu, Roxana Silbert and Ellen McDougall. Freelance work includes BAFTA-winning CBBC series *DIXI* (casting first three series). Nadine also has a long-running association as Casting Director for Synergy Theatre Project and is a full member of the Casting Directors' Guild.

JACK GREENYER | PRODUCTION MANAGER

Jack recently completed his training on the Royal Central School of Speech and Drama's BA Theatre Practice: Technical and Production Management course. He has since been working with theatre companies such as Complicité, National Youth Theatre, The Yard, Soho Theatre, tiata fahodzi, Up In Arms and Big House Theatre Company. Jack continues his commitment to help creative practitioners make the most of their spaces through his work with his company, Infinity Technical & Production Services

KATIE BACHTLER | STAGE MANAGER

Katie's theatre productions as Company Stage Manager and Stage Manager on Book include: *The Hoes* (Hampstead Theatre); *Fabric* (Damsel Productions, Soho Theatre, London); *Big Aftermath of a Small Disclosure* (ATC, Summerhall, Edinburgh Fringe); *A New and Better You* (The Yard); *Grotty* (Damsel Productions, Bunker Theatre, London); *Winter Solstice* (ATC, UK tour); *Dear Brutus* (Southwark Playhouse, London). She was Technical Stage Manager at Assembly Festival as part of the Edinburgh Festival Fringe. Events include Gibson Street Gala (Glasgow); Kentish Town Community Festival (London) and the annual Glasgow Film Festival as Venue Coordinator. Katie trained at Edinburgh Stage Management School and completed an MA in English Literature and Theatre Studies at the University of Glasgow.

Soho Theatre is London's most vibrant venue for new theatre, comedy and cabaret. We occupy a unique and vital place in the British cultural landscape. Our mission is to produce new work, discover and nurture new writers and artists, and target and develop new audiences. We work with artists in a variety of ways, from full producing of new plays, to co-producing new work, working with associate artists and presenting the best new emerging theatre companies that we can find.

We have numerous artists on attachment and under commission, including Soho Six and a thriving Young Company of writers and comedy groups. We read and see hundreds of scripts and shows a year.

'The place was buzzing, and there were queues all over the building as audiences waited to go into one or other of the venue's spaces... exuberant and clearly anticipating a good time.' Guardian.

We attract over 240,000 audience members a year at Soho Theatre, at festivals and through our national and international touring. We produced, co-produced or staged over 40 new plays in the last 12 months.

As an entrepreneurial charity and social enterprise, we have created an innovative and sustainable business model. We maximise value from Arts Council England and philanthropic funding, contributing more to government in tax and NI than we receive in public funding.

Registered Charity No: 267234

Soho Theatre, 21 Dean Street
London W1D 3NE
Admin 020 7287 5060
Box Office 020 7478 0100

OPPORTUNITIES FOR WRITERS AT SOHO THEATRE

We are looking for unique and unheard voices – from all backgrounds, attitudes and places.

We want to make things you've never seen before.

Alongside workshops, readings and notes sessions, there are several ways writers can connect with Soho Theatre. You can

· **enter** our prestigious biennial competition the **Verity Bargate Award** just as **Vicky Jones** did in 2013 with her Award-winning first play *The One*.

· **participate** in our nine month long **Writers' Labs programme**, where we will take you through a three-draft process.

- **submit** your script to submissions@sohotheatre.com where your play will go directly to our Artistic team

- **invite** us to see your show via coverage@sohotheatre.com

We consider every submission for production or any of the further development opportunities.

sohotheatre.com

Keep up to date:

sohotheatre.com
@sohotheatre all social media

SUPPORTERS

Principal Supporters
Nicholas Allott OBE
Hani Farsi
Hedley and
    Fiona Goldberg
Jack and Linda Keenan
Amelia and Neil Mendoza
Lady Susie Sainsbury
Carolyn Ward
Jennifer and
    Roger Wingate

Supporting Partners
Dean Attew
Jo Bennett-Coles
Tamara Box
Moyra Doyle
Stephen Garrett
Beatrice Hollond
Angela Hyde-Courtney
Garry Watts

Corporate Supporters
Adnams Southwold
Bargate Murray
Bates Wells & Braithwaite
Cameron Mackintosh Ltd
Character Seven
EPIC Private Equity
Financial Express
Fosters
The Groucho Club
John Lewis Oxford Street
Latham & Watkins LLP
Lionsgate UK
The Nadler Hotel
Oberon Books Ltd
Overbury Leisure
Quo Vardis
Richmond Associates
Soho Estates
Soundcraft

Trusts & Foundations
The Andor Charitable Trust
The Austin and Hope
Pilkington Charitable Trust
Backstage Trust
Bertha Foundation
Bruce Wake Charitable
    Trust
The Boris Karloff
    Charitable Foundation
The Boshier-Hinton
    Foundation
The Buzzacott Stuart
    Defries Memorial Fund

Chapman Charitable Trust
The Charles Rifkind and
    Jonathan Levy
    Charitable Settlement
The Charlotte Bonham-
    Carter Charitable Trust
Cockayne – Grants for the
    Arts and The London
    Community Foundation
John S Cohen Foundation
The Coutts Charitable
    Trust
The David and Elaine
    Potter Foundation
The D'Oyly Carte
    Charitable Trust
The 8th Earl of Sandwich
    Memorial Trust
The Edward Harvist Trust
The Eranda Rothschild
    Foundation
The Ernest Cook Trust
Esmée Fairbairn
    Foundation
The Fenton Arts Trust
Fidelio Charitable Trust
The Foundation for Sport
    and the Arts
Foyle Foundation
Garrick Charitable Trust
The Goldsmiths' Company
The Late Mrs Margaret
    Guido's Charitable Trust
Harold Hyam Wingate
    Foundation
Help A London Child
Hyde Park Place Estate
    Charity
The Ian Mactaggart Trust
The Idlewild Trust
The John Thaw
    Foundation
John Ellerman Foundation
John Lewis Oxford Street
Community Matters
Scheme
John Lyon's Charity
JP Getty Jnr Charitable
    Trust
The Kobler Trust
The Leche Trust
The Mackintosh
    Foundation
Mohamed S. Farsi
    Foundation
Noël Coward Foundation
The Peggy Ramsay
    Foundation
The Rose Foundation

The Royal Victoria Hall
    Foundation
Santander Foundation
Schroder Charity Trust
St Giles-in-the-Fields and
    William Shelton
    Educational Charity
The St James's Piccadilly
    Charity
Tallow Chandlers
    Benevolent Fund
The Teale Charitable Trust
The Theatres Trust
The Thistle Trust
Unity Theatre Charitable
    Trust
The Wolfson Foundation

Soho Theatre
Performance Friends
Matthew Bunting
Anya Hindmarch and
    James Seymour
Isobel and Michael Holland
David King
Gary Kemp
Steve and Diane Kordas
Andrew Lucas
Lady Caroline Mactaggart
Ian Ritchie and Jocelyne
    van den Bossche
Mark Whiteley
Gary Wilder
Hilary and Stuart Williams
Patrick Woodroffe

Soho Theatre
Playwright Friends
David Aukin
Natalie Bakova
Jim Boyle
Fiona Dewar
Manu Duggal
Anthony Eaton
Denzil and Renate
    Fernandez
Dominic Flynn
Jonathan Glanz and
    Manuela Raimondo
Alban Gordon
Andrew Gregory
Fawn James
John James
Shappi Khorsandi
Jeremy King OBE
David and Linda Lakhdhir
Jonathan Levy
David Macmillan
Adam Morley
Phil and Jane Radcliff

Sue Robertson
Dan Ross
Chantel Sinclair-Gray
Lesley Symons
Andrea Wong
Matt Woodford
Henry Wyndham
Christopher Yu

**Soho Theatre
Comedy Friends**
Tiffany Agbeko
Oladipo Agboluaje
Fran Allen
Marwan Alrasheed
Katherine Andreen
Adele Ashton
James Atkinson
Polly Balsom
Adam Barnes
Patrick Barrett
Zarina Bart
Uri Baruchin
Antonio Batista
Katie Battock
Ben Battcock
David Bend
Cody Benoy
Georgia Bird
Kieran Birt
Peter Bottomley
Matthew Boyle
James Brew
Christian Braeker
Rajan Brotia
Christie Brown
Joni Browne
Jesse Buckle
Iain Burnett
Indigo Carnie
Chris Carter
Paul Chard
Camilla Cole
Roisin Conaty
Vanessa Cook
Grant Court
Josephine Curry
Haralambos Dayantis
Sharon Eva Degen
Laura Denholm
Niki di Palma
Jeff Dormer
Kate Emery
Paul Entwistle
Amanda Farley
Samantha Fennessy
Peter Fenwick
Sue Fletcher

Stephen Fowler
Nick Fox
Cyrus Gilbert-Rolfe
Jake Godfrey
Terry Good
Robert Grant
Eva Greenspan
Steven Greenwood
Emma Gunnell
Edward Hacking
Gary Haigh
Irene Hakansson
John Hamilton
Colin Hann
Tim Harding
Anthony Hawser
Gillian Holmes
Karen Howlett
Georgia Ince
John Ireland
Alice Jefferis
Nadia Jennings
Nicola Johnson
Jo Jolley
Toby Jones
Anthony Kehoe
Robert King
Julie Knight
Andreas Kubat
Michael Kunz
Clive Laing
Simon Lee
Ian Livingston
Lucy Lumsden
Marea Maloney
Amanda Mason
Neil Mastrarrigo
Douglas McIlroy
Lauren McLardie
Roy Mclean
Chris McQuiggin
Jennifer Meech
Laura Meecham
Lauren Meehan
Kosten Metreweli
Mike Miller
Ryan Miller
Nick Mills
Robert Mitchell
Richard Moore
Maryam Mossavar
Mr and Mrs Roger
Myddelton
James Nicoll
Alan Pardoe
Simon Parsonage
Curro Perez Alcantara
Andrew Perkins

Keith Petts
Nick Pontt
Helena Prytz
Ashwin Rattan
Paul Rogers
Antonia Rolph
Graeme Rossiter
Rebecca Rycroft
Natalia Siabkin
Michelle Singer
Hari Sriskantha
Sarah Stanford
Jennifer Stott
Daniel Taylor
Andrew Thorne
Anthony Stewart Townson
Domenico Veronese
Rocco Vogel
Gabriel Vogt
Zachary Webb
Mike Welsh
Matt Whitehurst
Alexandra Williams
Gareth Williams
Kevin Williams
Allan Willis
Kirsten Wilson
Maria Wray
Liz Young

Soho Theatre has the
support of the Channel 4
Playwrights' Scheme
sponsored by Channel 4
Television.

We are also supported by
Westminster City Council
West End Ward Budget
and the London Borough
of Waltham Forest.

*We would also like to
thank those supporters
who wish to remain
anonymous*

soft animals

Holly Robinson

Acknowledgements

The making of *soft animals* has, in many ways, felt like the making of me. I'm so grateful to all the people who have shown kindness to me or the play in the last two years.

Isabella James, Siân Maxwell, Jeremy Franklin, Daniel Wye, Lily Hall, Jonathan Case, Dominik Kurzeja, Liam Bessell, Elizabeth Court, Emily Holt, Olivia Dent, A.M. Spier and family, Sian Brooke, Jacoba Williams, Cherrelle Skeete, Fiona Button, Anna Himali Howard, Charlotte Fraser, Soho Writers Alumni 2017/18, Iman Qureshi & Caitlin McEwan, Geraldine Lang, Ifeyinwa Frederick, Emma Bentley, Andy Stumps, Jules Haworth, Roy Williams, E. Mitchell and Katie Mitchell, Alice Birch, Amy Ball, Jay Miller, Lara Tysselling, Ashleigh Wheeler, Nick Hern Books and the wonderful Kirsten Foster.

This production would have been an impossibility without, of course, the magic cast and crew. The magnificent Bianca Stephens and Ellie Piercy, Holly De Angelis and David Luff, Anna Reid and Anna Clock and Ali Hunter, Katie Bachtler, Jack Greenyer, Nadine Rennie and all the Soho Team.

The play itself would have been an impossibility without the belief, care, frustratingly excellent notes and endless help of Lakesha Arie-Angelo and Adam Brace. They were the first people to make me feel like a Writer – a gift beyond measure. Every page that follows contains some (and often many) marks of their brilliance.

My writing would be an impossibility without the magic of Playbox Theatre Company (Emily Quash, Mary King, Stewart McGill, Juliet Vankay), who taught me what theatre can be and how to be an artist and a person, as well as gifting me with the best people in my life. I, especially, wouldn't be half the Theatre Tiger I am without knowing the genius brain of Toby Quash. Salutes.

I would be an impossibility without Stephanie Young, Mary Lynch and Charlotte Merriam, without George Fletcher and without my parents.

Steph, thank you for being that flatmate of our dreams. Mary, thank you for being My Person. Merriam, thank you for being the JM to my Silv.

Fletch, my first and best reader, thank you for the glorious everything of you.

Mum and Dad – 121 reallys. Thank you for every single one.

H.R.

*

For all the women I have loved in all the ways
I have loved them.

'You do not have to be good.
You do not have to walk on your knees
for a hundred miles through the desert repenting.
You only have to let the soft animal of your body
love what it loves.
Tell me about despair, yours, and I will tell you mine.'

'Wild Geese', Mary Oliver

6

Characters

SARAH, *late thirties, white*
FRANKIE, *nineteen/twenty, black, from Birmingham*

Note on Play

The action mainly takes place in Sarah's living room in her small, stylish house in Fulham. The stage should not look like a living room.

It's somewhere a baby used to live. She does not live here any more.

The action need almost never be literal. Props (with the exception of probably the teddy bears and talcum powder) do not need to manifest. The car can be a pool of light. Each time Sarah and Frankie touch, it must in some way be staged but, for example, where is says Frankie paints Sarah's nails – she might just hold her hand.

In transitions, we might see Sarah putting on the coat, doing her hair up. We might see Frankie alone in her room, holding the teddies or examining her scar.

There are about a load of teddy bears – not hidden but not seen – around the space, that Sarah will retrieve. They are the kind of things you find in gift shops around London, tacky and ridiculous but it's pretty impossible to say no when your child asks for one.

There is a crib somewhere on stage.

The crib is not centre-stage.

* indicates a time/place shift.

# indicates a pause.

/ indicates an interruption.

Lines in [square brackets] should not be read and are just to indicate an unfinished thought.

This text went to press before the end of rehearsals and so may differ slightly from the play as performed.

1.

February.

Outside SARAH*'s house in Fulham, London. The word 'cunt' has been spray-painted across her front door – we probably don't see this.*

FRANKIE *is stood outside the front door. Deciding whether to knock. Transfixed by the graffiti.*

SARAH *comes out.*

SARAH. Did you do this?

FRANKIE. Sorry?

SARAH. This, did you do / it?

FRANKIE. No.

SARAH. Right.

FRANKIE. Really. Really. I.

SARAH. My neighbour says you've been lingering –

FRANKIE. I was – just –

SARAH. Loitering, actually, she said loitering. Which seems / somewhat [loaded].

FRANKIE. I was – just –

SARAH. She hasn't spoken to me in four months and sixteen days. But now there's an obscenity on the front door –

 You didn't do it?

FRANKIE. Spray-paint uh –

SARAH. Cunt?

FRANKIE. On your front door? No, I really did not.

 Are you going to get rid of it?

SARAH. I think I might keep it. Adds value to the property. Cheaper than a conservatory.

FRANKIE. It looks like it's still wet. The sooner you –

SARAH (*waves her hands, her nails are drying*). Can't anyway. Big meeting.

FRANKIE. Are you uh going to call the police?

SARAH. Over a little paint?

FRANKIE. It's – it's not a little paint.

SARAH. Are you a journalist?

FRANKIE. No?

SARAH. Because I'm not talking to journalists.

FRANKIE. I'm not a journalist?

SARAH. Are you sure? You don't sound sure.

FRANKIE. I am. Sure. That I'm not. A journalist.

SARAH. If you're here about the house I will scream.

FRANKIE. I'm not here about the house.

SARAH. Okay.

FRANKIE. Sorry. Actually. I'm. We've. Actually. We've –

SARAH. We've what?

FRANKIE. I'm Frankie?

SARAH (*realises*). Frankie.

FRANKIE. From –

SARAH. Yes.

Of course.

Your arm?

FRANKIE. Yes. It. It healed.

SARAH. Do you want to come in then, Frankie?

*

They are inside. They don't really have anything to say to each other.

SARAH. Would you like a   FRANKIE. That's a lot of
cup of tea?   post.

I haven't been opening it, since?

FRANKIE. No, I'm okay, thank you.

SARAH. You're meant to say yes.

FRANKIE. Oh, okay. Um yes.

SARAH. Okay. Milk? Sugar?

FRANKIE. Are your nails dry?

SARAH. Oh. No. I should let them dry. Big meeting.

FRANKIE. What's the / meeting?

SARAH. So why are you here?

FRANKIE. Um.

SARAH. Were you not expecting me to ask?

FRANKIE. Do you ever get on the Tube and you don't know
where you're going and you just end up –

SARAH. In Fulham?

FRANKIE. Sorry. Is this totally inappropriate? This is totally
inappropriate. I don't know why I thought this was –

I just wanted to. I wanted to see you again.

SARAH. When you've got a baby, you don't just end up
anywhere. It sounds… nice.

I still haven't made your tea.

FRANKIE. Your nails.

SARAH. You make it. The tea bags are next to the bread bin, on
the left.

FRANKIE. Okay.

I don't actually like tea.

SARAH. Then why did you say you wanted one?

FRANKIE. You said I was meant to.

SARAH. I was – joking. It was. You don't have to just because –

FRANKIE. I wasn't. I really wasn't.

SARAH. You can go.

She doesn't.

FRANKIE. You smudged your nails.

SARAH. Shit.

I'm awful at it. I normally go to the salon but my usual girl weeps every time she sees me.

#

FRANKIE. I could do it for you?

Like only if you wanted.

SARAH. That's [a strange thing to offer].

FRANKIE. I'm good. Not like. I can't like draw animals on them or anything. But one coat. Easy.

SARAH. No. It's fine.

FRANKIE. It's no bother.

SARAH. I can do it myself.

FRANKIE. I'm not doing anything else.

SARAH. I still don't really know why you're here.

FRANKIE. Yeah. Nor do I.

But while I am –

#

SARAH. Okay.

FRANKIE *paints* SARAH*'s nails – or she just holds her hand – either way they touch. It is the first time either of*

them have touched or been touched with care in months. It is
unbearably intimate.

Are you going to cry?

FRANKIE. No.

SARAH. You look different.

FRANKIE. I put on some weight, I think. And my hair is
[different – *this can be more specific to the actor's hairstyle*].

SARAH. I don't want you to think I didn't recognise you
because you're black.

FRANKIE. I didn't think that. It was – you weren't focused
on me.

SARAH. No.

FRANKIE. But white people never recognise me. They always
think I'm the other black girl they know. Literally none of
my tutors at uni know who I am. To be fair, that might be
because I never go lectures but.

SARAH. What do you do instead? Party?

FRANKIE. Sleep.

SARAH. Oh. What do you study?

FRANKIE. Theology.

SARAH. Theology?

FRANKIE. Yeah. What do you do? Are you back at work?

SARAH. No. I don't know what I do.

     #

FRANKIE. Done.

SARAH. Thank you.

     #

FRANKIE. I should let you get off to your meeting. I need to –

SARAH. Do you want to come?

FRANKIE. To your meeting?

SARAH. It's with my divorce lawyer.

FRANKIE. I've got to go –

SARAH. Or we could just end up somewhere!

FRANKIE. I really can't.

SARAH. No. Sorry. Of course.

FRANKIE. It's not that – I just.

SARAH. What?

FRANKIE. I promised to ring my nan.

SARAH. Oh, fuck your nan.

Sorry.

FRANKIE. I could come back.

SARAH. Yes?

FRANKIE. Yeah?

SARAH. You don't have to say yes just because my daughter is dead.

FRANKIE. Yeah, I know. Good luck – for your meeting.

SARAH. Yes.

FRANKIE. Sarah, you shouldn't. You shouldn't let him take all the stuff just because –

SARAH. I wasn't planning on, Frankie.

2.

A few days later. SARAH*'s house.*

FRANKIE *has handed over a bottle of graffiti-remover liquid.*

FRANKIE. It's pretty strong, I spilt some in my room and it still reeks. But the guy in the shop said it would strip anything off anything.

SARAH. You didn't have to.

FRANKIE. Yeah. Well.

SARAH. I wasn't sure you'd come back.

FRANKIE. You said I could.

SARAH. No, I know. I got something for you too, actually.

FRANKIE. For me?

SARAH. I went to the zoo. After my meeting, well, during. I walked out. Steven thinks he can sell the house, this house. Which. I decided to just get on the Tube and end up somewhere. Like you said. I ended up at the zoo. I got you this.

  SARAH *gives* FRANKIE *a lemur teddy.*

FRANKIE. What is it?

SARAH. A lemur.

FRANKIE (*unsure if she's missed the joke*). The ones that kill themselves?

SARAH. That's lemmings.

FRANKIE. Oh.

SARAH. And this is a lemur.

FRANKIE. Right.

SARAH. And they don't. Actually.

FRANKIE. Don't?

SARAH. Kill themselves. Lemmings. It's a myth. There was an article in the *Sunday Times Magazine*. But this. This is a lemur, anyway.

FRANKIE. A lemur. No one. No one's ever given me a lemur before.

SARAH. I was in the gift shop and I found myself thinking about you and I just. This is ridiculous / isn't it?

FRANKIE. It's amazing. Thank you.

SARAH. Do you want a drink?

FRANKIE. Okay. Yes.

SARAH. Not tea?

FRANKIE. Not tea.

SARAH. Coffee?

FRANKIE. I'm trying not to. Water?

They are both trying to think of something to say.

SARAH. How's university?

FRANKIE. Did anyone recognise you at the zoo? Sorry – is that?

SARAH. No. I thought one man by the giraffes might have done. They do out and about sometimes. Around here, everyone knows who I am.

FRANKIE. Do they – say anything?

SARAH. It's dying down. The first two months were ridiculous. The press were everywhere and wherever we went there would be something. In the sixth week, this mum slapped me in the park. Steven called the police. After I was on *Good Morning Britain*, someone threw a brick through the window.

It's normally stares, muttered comments, the occasional... heckle. I can't go into Sainsbury's, too many teenagers. I have to shop at the little Waitrose by the Tube. Quite a shock to my monthly budget. It's been quiet though recently. I thought it would stay – worse.

  #

FRANKIE. They'd recognise you if your hair was up.

SARAH. Hm?

FRANKIE. The picture they used everywhere. Your hair was up.

SARAH. You mean the mugshot?

FRANKIE. Sorry. That was really. Sorry. God. I'm just –

SARAH. It's fine.

  #

Do you have a scar? On your arm?

FRANKIE. Yes.

SARAH. Can I see?

  FRANKIE shows her. SARAH holds her arm tentatively.

It's still – Are you putting anything on it?

FRANKIE. No.

SARAH. I have some Bio-Oil. Helped with my stretch marks.

FRANKIE. You don't look like you've stretched a day in
    your life.

SARAH. Well – pregnancy.

FRANKIE. Oh.

Did your feet get any bigger? I read that the other day. That
some women's feet get bigger and never go back.

SARAH. Mine grew two sizes. Played havoc with my Manolo
    Blahnik collection.

FRANKIE. Fuck.

  FRANKIE stares at her feet.

SARAH. I was joking, Frankie.

FRANKIE. About your feet?

SARAH. No, I don't own any Manolos. My feet are still huge.

FRANKIE. Well you know what they say about big feet.

SARAH. Big socks?

FRANKIE. Massive clitoris.

SARAH *bursts out laughing*.

SARAH. I haven't laughed like that in months.

FRANKIE. Sorry.

SARAH. You keep saying that. I've missed it.

I'll get you that Bio-Oil. It works best if you apply it twice a day.

FRANKIE. Do you want to sort out the Banksy? The guy in the shop said there would be a tutorial on YouTube.

SARAH. This is silly, you're – I'm sure you've got reading to do and new and exciting university friends. You shouldn't be googling how to get rid of graffiti.

FRANKIE. And what will you do?

SARAH. I –

FRANKIE. So far the closest thing I have to a friend is Lucy from Portsmouth who keeps making me cups of tea in the hope I'll forget she got fingered by a lacrosse player on our communal kitchen table during freshers'.

SARAH *smiles*.

SARAH. And you don't like tea.

FRANKIE. I don't like tea.

FRANKIE *smiles*.

SARAH. Okay.

FRANKIE. Okay.

SARAH *takes the fluid off* FRANKIE. *She smiles.*
FRANKIE *grins. A beginning.*

3.

A teddy with a ruff has joined the ranks. SARAH *sits with a dinosaur teddy on her lap.* FRANKIE *is plaiting her hair.*

SARAH. I've been wearing my hair up and everyone's been staring. Not like half 'do I know you' glances. Completely just 'you're her'.

FRANKIE. It wasn't [a suggestion].

SARAH. These girls at the museum – shoved past me right by the whale – they definitely knew who I was. I thought one of them had her / phone out which

FRANKIE. It wasn't a suggestion. Sarah. I wasn't telling you to put on the same coat and...

SARAH*'s eyes light up.*

Sarah. No. Don't do that.

SARAH. Ow.

FRANKIE. Point your chin down.

SARAH. How was your tutor meeting?

FRANKIE. He said I've got to get my attendance up. Last term, I wasn't really on it. It's fine. First year doesn't count-count. I just have to pass.

SARAH. Were you unwell?

FRANKIE. No.

SARAH. If you don't want to / say that's

FRANKIE. Well. The – accident, happened right at the start of term and um, threw me and I didn't really catch up. And I was a bit –

SARAH. Right.

FRANKIE. So my tutors said –

SARAH. Right.

> #

> I'm sorry.

FRANKIE. Oh my god. No, of course, no. Sarah, please, I didn't say. I just wanted to be – honest? I was already a mess right from when I got here. Not going in, doing stupid stuff.

SARAH. No. It's nice. No one tells me the truth any more. No one says anything remotely selfish to me. My sister-in-law didn't tell me about a cancer scare. Steven, kept pretending it was fine. That he didn't blame me. That he wasn't angry and hurting and that he didn't hate me. And it ate us alive those three months. And now I have meetings with lawyers.

FRANKIE. Keep your head still. Are you angry at him?

SARAH. About the house, furious. But I don't blame him for leaving me. I would have left him. I would have left me. I wouldn't have lasted as long as he did even. He deserves credit.

FRANKIE. Do you miss him?

SARAH. No. Not the himness of him, you know. He was my husband but it was sort of like –

You know how people have dogs and they love their dogs and they take photos of them and buy them jumpers and cry when they die and you all have to chip in money at work to buy them flowers even though it was just a fucking Pomeranian. Steve was like a dog. I loved him. I love him. I do. But he was like a Labrador and, in reality, if at the pet shop, I'd gone for a, I don't know, a King Charles Spaniel, instead, I would have loved that just as much. We loved each other because that's what people do they love their dogs and their husbands.

It's just the – ease that I miss. I don't miss him or need him but when I come back to this [empty house]. All I want to do is order a curry. And I don't know what my favourite curry is. He did the ordering in. He must have had the number memorised or on his phone or –

There was this one curry. It's lamb with this yogurt and it's just the right kind of spicy. I used to be able to handle vindaloo but after – when I was pregnant, I went completely off it but this one was just right. Not too greasy. And the naan too – not too thick. I tried to order it last week from one of those apps. But it wasn't the right one. It was all creamy and thick and wrong. I just want to ring him and say 'Hey, I know you hate me, I know it's my fault she's gone but please, which is the good curry house, what's the curry I like, with the lamb called? Thank you, Steven. Goodnight.' That's all I want.

#

Is it strange?

FRANKIE. What?

SARAH. Being here. With me.

FRANKIE. I think it's strange how not-strange it is.

SARAH. Do you tell anyone?

FRANKIE. Do you tell anyone I'm here?

SARAH. Ha. Like who?

FRANKIE. Friends?

SARAH. They've all disappeared.

FRANKIE. Family? What about your parents?

SARAH. Gone. I don't have anyone left to tell.

FRANKIE. No one knows, actually, about me.

SARAH. No one knows what?

FRANKIE. That I was there. That I was – that I broke the window. I mean my tutors and the doctors but I didn't tell anyone real.

SARAH. That can't be healthy. No one knowing. Having no one to talk to about it.

FRANKIE. I don't see you going to group therapy.

SARAH. I was invited to one actually.

FRANKIE. Sorry.

SARAH. Steven found one in America. They have thirty-eight cases on average a year, so. He showed me the website with

all these clip-art angels and heart-wrenching testimonies.
And all I could think was how fucking tacky do you have to
be to put clip art on a website memorial for your dead son.

I suppose that makes me a terrible person.

FRANKIE. No.

SARAH. Really?

FRANKIE. Not as bad as the killing-your-baby part.

That was. [Shit.] I'm sorry.

SARAH *laughs*.

SARAH. Relax, Frankie. That was funny. That was really funny.

It's always like this, me confessing to you some terrible
thing I've done. But then I suppose we're only here because
of some terrible thing I've done so –

FRANKIE. I ruined my English teacher's marriage.

SARAH. That's more like it. How?

FRANKIE. I emailed his wife and told her he was having an
affair...

He wasn't but I knew enough to make it look like he was.
Turned out she'd been looking for an excuse to go. Took the
kids. He only sees them every third weekend.

SARAH. Why?

FRANKIE. She got custody.

SARAH. [No.] Why did you do it?

FRANKIE. We were like friends. Whenever the other kids were
being shit, he would give me this look like 'Can you see what
I have to deal with?' Like we had a, not a secret, but we were
on a level. The teachers didn't really like me at school. I was
really clever but bored so I got a bit mouthy. Mr Taylor told
me to read *Jane Eyre*, I told him to watch *Orange is the New
Black*. I was his favourite. Then when I was in Year 11, I won
this poetry competition. He drove me over to Oxford to get
my prize. He told me I belonged there, somewhere like that.

Somewhere away from Bearwood, from Birmingham.
It was one of the best days of my life.

And then in the car on the way home, he said I was more
important than I'd ever know, put his hand on my knee and
leant in.

Except he didn't do it. He didn't kiss me. He changed his
mind, realised what a creep he was being and he stopped.

And it ruined everything.

SARAH. He was your teacher. / He was meant to stop.

FRANKIE. I know.

SARAH. You were – what – fifteen? He wasn't even meant to
let it / get that far. Jesus.

FRANKIE. But he did. He let it. He let it get that far. He was
the only person who made me feel clever and – valuable and
he, he, he took it away in an instant. All of it. And I was
fifteen and angry and clever so I ruined his marriage.

SARAH. Did he know it was you?

FRANKIE. No. He cried to me about it after my English GCSE
Language. Held my hand. Then he said we 'shouldn't be
alone any more'.

SARAH. Fucking hell.

FRANKIE. Sometimes, I wish he'd kissed me. I know that's…
I know that's fucked. And that would have fucked me up in
seventeen other ways but there's words for that. I know it
would have been – but I do think it would have made me feel
so much less [alone]. I wouldn't have felt so –

SARAH. Are you still in touch?

FRANKIE. We're Facebook friends. He posts about fathers'
rights. I do feel guilty.

SARAH. Fucking hell.

      #

Shall I do your hair now?

FRANKIE. As a general rule, I don't let white women touch my hair.

SARAH *throws one of the bears at her*.

We could open the post.

SARAH. I'd really rather not.

FRANKIE. It's piling up, Sarah.

SARAH. It's boring.

FRANKIE. We should just get it over with.

SARAH. Why?

FRANKIE. So you don't suffocate under it.

SARAH. Where should I go tomorrow? I was thinking the Tower of London – where I belong according to some online commentators.

FRANKIE. You shouldn't read that stuff.

SARAH. No.

FRANKIE. But you do.

SARAH. Yeah.

4.

The next week. SARAH*'s flat. A Beefeater teddy has joined the ranks. And today's – a robot teddy.*

SARAH *and* FRANKIE *are opening* SARAH*'s post.* FRANKIE *returns from the loo.*

Throughout the scene they open and discard many letters. Some are horrendous, some benign, some kind, some are bills or spam.

SARAH. Have you got a UTI?

FRANKIE. What?

SARAH. That was the third time this afternoon.

FRANKIE. Who are you? The urine police?

SARAH. According to this one I'm a modern-day Medea.
    Which one was Medea?

FRANKIE. Jason's wife. She killed and ate her children.

SARAH. Charming.

    #

FRANKIE. This one's a bill.

    #

SARAH. This one is praying for me.

FRANKIE. I'm surprised how many – nice ones there are.

SARAH. I do have well-wishers. I got a lot of flowers in the
    early days.

FRANKIE. You only talk about the bad stuff.

SARAH. You only ask about the bad stuff.

    The sympathy is the bad stuff anyway.

FRANKIE. This one is about the house.

SARAH. Bin that.

FRANKIE. It looks serious. He can't sell it while you're still
    here, right?

SARAH. No.

FRANKIE. That no sounded like a yes.

SARAH. Amanda wants to bring back hanging for little old me.

FRANKIE. A lot of them reference the last interview… When you said 'I'm not looking for forgiveness.'

She waits for SARAH *to say something, she doesn't.*

I just thought, when I read it, that you were going to be –

SARAH. Less Ice Queen Who Boiled Her Baby?

FRANKIE. Can you not?

SARAH. Sorry, Frankie, am I upsetting you?

FRANKIE. Forget it. I just thought you'd be a little softer.

FRANKIE opens a letter and before she can stop herself makes a small sad noise. She immediately balls up the letter and goes to throw it away.

SARAH. What's that one?

FRANKIE. Nothing.

SARAH. Frankie?

FRANKIE. Just a bill.

SARAH. A bill – you're sighing over a bill? Give it here. Frankie, it's my post.

FRANKIE. It's from the – the GP.

SARAH. Yes? Do I need a smear test?

FRANKIE. It was scheduling in her eighteen-month check-up.

SARAH. Oh.

Some moments pass. They open more letters, discarding, passing them over to read.

They open more.

FRANKIE. Sarah, this one is really grim. He's threatening you like explicitly and specifically and. He's left his name, Adam. It's signed Adam. Fucking hell.

FRANKIE *hands the letter over.*

SARAH. 'I'll hurt you like you hurt her. Atone.' Positively biblical.

FRANKIE. You need to – to show it to the police. These are explicit threats. It's got his name and phone number. They can arrest him or caution him or something. Sarah? Yes?

SARAH. Mhm.

FRANKIE. Are you going to call them?

SARAH. When you've gone, yes. Be a shame to ruin all the fun we're having.

FRANKIE. You're so annoying.

This one is nice. Okay, okay. The sympathy is bad stuff.

Once FRANKIE *is engrossed in reading the kind letter,* SARAH *pockets the letter from Adam. It is clear she has no intention of showing it to the police.*

SARAH. This one is verging on a marriage proposal. I guess, Myra wouldn't have him.

FRANKIE. You are technically single, you know.

SARAH. True. Though, it's not like I can get on – Tinder.

FRANKIE. Oh my god. Please can I put you on Tinder? We can use a different name! You have to see it, it's –

SARAH. Absolutely not.

FRANKIE. It's so easy –

SARAH. Francheska – no.

SARAH *is back to opening post.*

FRANKIE. 'Francheska, no.' Are you my mum?

White powder pours from the envelope SARAH *was opening. Everything freezes. It's terrifying.*

Don't. Fuck. Fuck. Stay still. Fuck. I'll call –

FRANKIE can't find her phone. She does something like covers her mouth with her sleeve. SARAH sits stock-still.

Stay still. I can't find my phone. Where's your phone – where –

SARAH stickers her finger directly into the powder, lifts it to her mouth and licks it.

What!!

SARAH. It's talcum power.

FRANKIE. What are you doing –

SARAH. It's talc. Smell it.

FRANKIE. Oh my god.

SARAH. Fucking talcum powder.

SARAH begins to laugh. FRANKIE is relieved, then furious –

FRANKIE. Why did you – it could have been. I thought it was it was arsenic, anthrax.

SARAH. Talcum powder.

SARAH throws a handful in FRANKIE's face.

FRANKIE. What are you doing?

SARAH begins to throw the talc around. To fling it over FRANKIE and herself. FRANKIE watches first – and then joins in. There is more powder than could be in one envelope. Maybe it is in every envelope. The stage is littered, transformed, made beautiful. They pour it on themselves. In their hair. Smearing their faces. A ritual. The world is made of fake anthrax and they dance in it. They collapse.

SARAH. It smells like her. Talc. It smells like her. I wonder if that's why they did it.

FRANKIE. Are you okay?

SARAH. I'm fine.

FRANKIE (*quietly*). Sarah, it wasn't your fault.

> SARAH *doesn't acknowledge this.* FRANKIE *gets a make-up wipe from her bag or somewhere. She gives one to* SARAH *and goes to take one for herself.* SARAH *moves across to* FRANKIE. *She uses her wipe to clear the talc from* FRANKIE's *face.* FRANKIE *is, for a second, shocked by this new intimacy. Then she takes her wipe and does the same for* SARAH.

> *The moment hangs. And ends.*

How was the science museum?

SARAH. There was an animatronic baby robot.

FRANKIE. Yeah?

SARAH. Yeah.

FRANKIE. Shall we make you that Tinder profile then?

> *No attempt at a clear-up between scenes will ever fully rid the stage or the actors of talc. That is okay.*

5.

SARAH's *flat. A week or so later. Morning.* SARAH *is wearing the blue coat. Her hair is up.*

SARAH. I didn't know you were coming.

FRANKIE. Sorry, I know it's early, I really need to ask you about something – what are you wearing?

SARAH. My clothes.

FRANKIE. I've seen them before.

SARAH. Well. You're here a lot.

Do you want to come to the aquarium?

FRANKIE. You're. You're wearing the same coat. And your hair. And. You look like the photo. The mug – . That was a joke before, when I said you should wear the same clothes. Not even a joke.

SARAH. It was a mistake. I didn't realise.

FRANKIE. Sarah, is this how you've been going out?

SARAH. Frankie. Let me change.

SARAH *changes.*

The Sea Life Centre. Are you coming?

*

The aquarium – shown only through some kind of brilliant blue light. SARAH *and* FRANKIE *stand, watching things we can't see swim by. They don't speak. It's awkward. Being outside together isn't the same. Something is broken.*

SARAH. You – you wanted to ask me something earlier.

FRANKIE. It was nothing.

SARAH. Oh. Okay. Gift shop?

FRANKIE. I should go.

SARAH. Where?

FRANKIE. I have a seminar.

SARAH. Right. Good.

FRANKIE. Besides, it's not the same if I pick. See you.

SARAH. Yeah.

FRANKIE *leaves.* SARAH *is alone.*

6.

SARAH*'s flat. The following Tuesday.* SARAH *has given*
FRANKIE *a stingray toy.*

SARAH. I beat a teenage boy at air hockey, at the arcade,
afterwards and his friend said I was fit for a mum. Which
was depressing on multiple levels.

FRANKIE. Why do you keep going to all these touristy places?
It seems. It seems like it might be kind of reckless.

SARAH. I'm fine, Frankie. Really.

FRANKIE. Not for want of trying.

SARAH. This is meant to be for the estate agents but they can
go fuck themselves.

SARAH *gives* FRANKIE *a key.*

FRANKIE. A key?

SARAH. Yes.

FRANKIE. To here?

SARAH. Yes, Frankie. If you're here alone and anyone knocks
don't answer.

FRANKIE. Are people still coming round to hassle you?

SARAH. No, no. They're trying to show people around this
week. But they don't have a key. You do.

FRANKIE. I do.

SARAH. But you're not to come here instead of going to your
lectures.

FRANKIE. Okay.

SARAH. Have you been going?

FRANKIE. Yes.

SARAH. Really?

FRANKIE. I got my topic for the presentation thing for History
of Christianity. If I don't pass this, I might fail the year.

SARAH. What happens if you fail the year?

FRANKIE. I'd have to do first year again, from scratch and I. Do Not Think I could do that.

SARAH. And it was okay? Going in?

FRANKIE. I mean. Yes. But these girls, in my seminar group, were so shocked to see me. This one girl with private-school hair / literally

SARAH. Private-school hair?

FRANKIE. Oh *you* know – (*Swooshes her hair over.*) and they all have ridiculous names like Grisabella which they try and shorten to the least offensively posh version but it's like, I still know your hymen was broken by a horse. She was like 'Oh my god, oh my god, you're Frankie. Every week we play Frankie or no Frankie. And! This week! Frankie! Where are you every week?!'

And I just wanted to say 'I'm lying in my bed, not going outside because sometimes I feel certain if I go outside I'll throw myself in front of the first bus I see so it's much easier to sleep twenty hours a day then come in and listen to your regurgitated opinions on the Talmud, Pandora.

SARAH. I think it would be great, if you really tried to go in.

FRANKIE. I know. I am trying. I nearly quit in the second week. I was literally on my way when – uh. I will. Go in.

SARAH. When what? What were you going to say?

FRANKIE. That's when I found her.

SARAH. Oh.

FRANKIE. We don't have to talk about this.

SARAH. We haven't talked about this. I have no idea what happened to you that day. Isn't that funny?

FRANKIE. Did they not, did they not tell you during the investigation?

SARAH. I was the accused… You were *on your way* to quit?
    That afternoon? Why were you near my office? Where were
    you coming from?

FRANKIE. Someone's house.

SARAH. Someone?

FRANKIE. A guy. I was on my way to tell my personal tutor
    that I quit. And I was coming from this guy's house…

SARAH. Someone from Tinder?

FRANKIE. No.

SARAH. And you were at his and?

FRANKIE. Yes. Sarah –

SARAH. Please.

FRANKIE. Okay. Okay. I don't sleep over. Generally. I um leave
    after but I hadn't really been sleeping that week so I must have
    just [fallen asleep]. And I woke up in a panic in this
    unpleasantly hot room that smelt strange and tangy.

SARAH. Did you fuck again, then?

FRANKIE. No.

    Yes.

    I didn't really want to. But I did so. Which isn't. Not like
    that. I just.

    We don't have to talk about this.

SARAH. No, go on.

    *They are opening up something between them. A terrible
    wound they have been dancing around for a month.*

FRANKIE. We were uh [fucking]. And I realised it was
    Tuesday. And my tutor's office hours ended at two-thirty and
    it was like one-forty already because we'd slept so late and
    I was lying in this bed, being – and I thought. Fuck it. I quit.
    I don't want to be here, in this room, in this city, in this
    university, doing this big stupid thing I can't do with all

these girls who know Latin and know each other. So once he'd. I got dressed. I flipped my underwear. And left.

SARAH. And ended up by my office?

FRANKIE. My battery was on like two per cent and I realised I had no idea where I was so I Citymapped the route, screenshot it and put my phone on airplane mode and started walking. I was trying to get to this bus stop. And that's when I realised how – warm it was. It was the end of September and it was still so warm.

I did that thing where you think 'climate change' – (*Sort of shrugs*.) and I took my jacket off and kept walking but I was sweating – I remember because I was worried about smelling in the meeting.

And then my phone died. And I stopped and swore. And looked up. And then – and then.

SARAH. And then?

FRANKIE. I saw –

SARAH. Yes.

FRANKIE. I uh shouted for help but it was um. It's a side street, as you know and no one came. And my phone was dead.

SARAH. So you smashed the window?

FRANKIE. I put my shoe on my hand. I don't know why. I think I saw it on TV. I thought it would stop my hand from – breaking [?]. Then I used my elbow. It took. It took a few goes.

SARAH. Did it hurt?

FRANKIE. Yes. It really. I smashed the passenger window and I reached through. But I think I knew. Once I smashed the window and she didn't [react]. A bit of me knew. I tried to be very gentle. But her skin. It was. It sort of slipped.

I think that's when –

SARAH. You started screaming.

FRANKIE. Yes. And then you.

SARAH. Yes.

FRANKIE. I'd never seen – it was like you were on fire. Like someone had set you alight.

   #

SARAH. It's like snow on your eyelids.

   Have you not been skiing?

FRANKIE. Shockingly, no. I've never been skiing.

SARAH. Oh go fuck yourself, I went once at Exeter.

   It's blindingly bright out there with all the snow and sun. I didn't know I was meant to wear goggles – or my helmet for that matter. This was before – what's her name??

FRANKIE. Oh, um, um. The mum from *Parent Trap*. No, it's gone.

SARAH. I didn't wear my goggles and it was so bright. It meant that when it was actually snowing, I got this kind of retina burn. When I went inside. I could still see it snowing on the inside of my eyelids.

FRANKIE. Like after someone takes a photo with a flash.

SARAH. Yes, like that.

   It was like that. It's like that.

   I can see your arm bleeding on her. And I can see her skin slipping. I can see the colour of her. Her little body in your arms. Every time.

   I never really thought about it. During the investigation. I stopped thinking of you as a person. You were just this piece in the jigsaw of that day that I was trying to – (*Moves her hands to indicate putting something together.*) But you, you were very brave –

FRANKIE. No.

SARAH. Frankie. You saw her and you tried to help.

FRANKIE. This is the most you've talked about her. About what happened.

SARAH. I talked and talked and talked about it. The police. The TV stuff. The Swiss-fucking-cheese metaphor. I am so tired of hearing myself talk about memory, the hippocampus, the basal ganglia, the frontal cortex.

That's all anyone wants to know. How it happens. I don't know. I don't know how it happens.

This is what I know.

We all had colds. Steven took her in usually but he was worse. So I do. She is quiet in the back, drowsy. I sang to her. I liked to do that. There are roadworks. I drop her off at nursery. I joke with the nursery girl with the red hair about Paul Hollywood. I went to work. I had a good day. I was having a good day.

I got a new client. I'd just got off the call – and then we heard this screaming. Someone said something about my car. And then I was running downstairs and I thought 'I really need to go to the gym again, I've been so unfit since Rosie' and then I was outside and I saw you.

I saw you. I saw you. With your arms covered – . You smashed my car window. I thought you were trying to steal it. My car. Not because you're black. No, fuck it, maybe because you're black. I don't know. She was in your arms. And then. I realised, I'd dreamt up the conversation with the redhead. They call it false memory. I got to the roadworks and I turned into work like I always did and I came back five hours later. And it was September and it was so warm. Baking hot.

And then I knew.

What else is there to say? Hyperthermia and autolysis of the organs and everything, that's not what I know. What I know is you stood there, holding my girl in your arms.

There is a knock at the door. Then another. The knocks continue – because increasingly annoyed.

Shh. Shh. Sit down. They look through the windows.

They are crouched down, whispering.

FRANKIE. This is stupid, why don't you just / let them in?

SARAH. Because if someone sees this house they will buy it. And it is my house. It was her house.

They crouch. The knocking continues.

Where do you meet them?

FRANKIE. Who?

SARAH. The guys online.

FRANKIE. For real? This is what you want to talk about now?

The knocking intensifies. The agent calls 'Mrs Hargreave' through the door. Throughout the following conversation, SARAH *and* FRANKIE *look over their shoulders at the knocking. Occasionally quieting and then continuing to talk.*

SARAH. If they're not from Tinder – where? OkCupid?

FRANKIE. Craigslist.

SARAH. Craigslist? What kind of men meet women on craigslist?

FRANKIE. Not always the nicest.

SARAH. What kind of sex are you having?

FRANKIE. Not always the nicest.

SARAH. Tell me.

FRANKIE. I uh post ads and tell them they can do whatever they want to me.

SARAH. And what – what do they do?

FRANKIE. It's um, pretty bad.

SARAH. And you just go to these strangers' houses and just let them. Frankie. That doesn't sound – safe.

FRANKIE. Yeah.

Another burst of knocking/shouting. They're silent. It stops for a second.

SARAH. It's one thing, if you want, you know, rough stuff, BDSM whatever. Even anonymous stuff, I guess. That's all. There's no shame in that but you can be safe and do that. You can do it safely can't you?

FRANKIE. Probably.

SARAH. But you don't.

FRANKIE. No.

SARAH. When was the last time you / [did it?]

FRANKIE. Not since I've been coming here.

SARAH. Do you enjoy it?

FRANKIE. I don't want to enjoy it. I don't want to. I don't deserve –

SARAH. Oh Frankie. Sometimes. I just want to. You deserve to feel good.

SARAH takes FRANKIE's hands.

She kisses her fingertips. FRANKIE is confused but it's not that kind of kiss. She kisses her wrists. Her scar.

Then FRANKIE kisses SARAH on the lips. Like a lifeboat, like a kiss of life, like a spell. And then it ends.

He's gone.

The knocking has stopped.

FRANKIE. Natasha Richardson.

SARAH. Oh yeah. Liam Neeson's wife.

FRANKIE. I can't watch the bit, you know that bit in *Love Actually* where he cries in Emma Thompson's kitchen about his *Love Actually* wife being dead because now I just think about Natasha Richardson being actually dead –

SARAH. Oh god and Emma Thompson says no one ever's going to fancy you if you cry all the time –

FRANKIE. No one's ever going to shag you if you cry all the time.

Do you fancy me?

SARAH. I don't fancy you.

FRANKIE. I don't fancy you.

Thank you. You're the only person I talk to. Some days. Most days.

SARAH. You should call your mum.

7.

SARAH*'s flat. A few days later. A new teddy, with a judge's wig. Royal Courts of Justice.*

SARAH *and* FRANKIE *are tipsy.*

FRANKIE. I don't understand how all you have is wine.

SARAH. Wine is good.

FRANKIE. With a meal! With foie gras I'm sure / it's absolutely delightful

SARAH. How posh do you think / I am?!

FRANKIE. Not to get pissed off of. It makes my head hurt.

SARAH. That just means you need to drink more, Frankie.

FRANKIE. To finalised divorces! To me actually handing in an essay!

SARAH. To never having to suck his toes again!

FRANKIE. What the fuck – no!

SARAH. Oh yeah. I was kind of in to it in the beginning but then he started cycling everywhere / and

FRANKIE. That's nasty. Oh my god.

SARAH. No. No. I'm being cruel. He was a master at cunnilingus.

FRANKIE. Cunnilingus. Sometimes you talk like you're fifty-seven, you absolute freak.

Oh my god. Do you know how to play Never Have I Ever?

*

SARAH. Never have I ever um never have I ever ummmm –

FRANKIE. Come on!

SARAH. Got a tattoo.

Neither of them drink.

FRANKIE. Boring.

SARAH. Go on then!

FRANKIE. Never have I ever... done coke.

SARAH *drinks.* FRANKIE *does not.*

SARAH. At uni, twice. Disastrous. And then at the wedding of this boring woman from Steven's work. Michelle. One of those women who thinks liking gin is the same thing as having a personality. She had a sign at the reception that said gin o'clock.

FRANKIE. Who had the coke?

SARAH. Her little cousin.

FRANKIE. White people are fucking wild.

SARAH. Never have I ever had sex with a woman.

FRANKIE *drinks.* SARAH *does not.*

When? Who!

FRANKIE. A few times. I'm bisexual or whatever.

SARAH. Or whatever! I thought –

FRANKIE. I said I didn't fancy you not that I didn't fancy girls. I mainly fancy girls. Men are very mediocre.

SARAH. But. Do you do the thing. The bad-sex thing with women?

FRANKIE. Nah, women won't hurt you the way men will.

SARAH. Right.

Never have I ever fucked a married man.

FRANKIE drinks. SARAH drinks. FRANKIE is surprised.

Well my husband was technically married.

FRANKIE. Oh fuck you.

Never have I ever thought about killing myself.

SARAH. Well. That's a mother of a question.

FRANKIE. My rugby-playing flatmate posed it in freshers'.

SARAH. What a twat.

FRANKIE. Yeah.

They both drink.

SARAH. Never have I ever *tried* to kill myself.

Neither of them drinks.

Well, that's good.

FRANKIE. Well done us.

They burst out laughing.

SARAH. We got dark.

FRANKIE. Yeah.

SARAH. We always get dark.

FRANKIE. Yeah.

SARAH. I don't want to get dark. I want to get drunk.

FRANKIE. You are drunk.

SARAH. Let's go dancing!

FRANKIE. I don't think that's a good / idea, Sarah

SARAH. It's a great idea!

FRANKIE. All the people, Sarah –

SARAH. You are so boring sometimes. We never go anywhere. You're young. I'm – I'm divorced. We're going.

FRANKIE. I don't have anything to wear.

SARAH. I have clothes. You can wear my clothes. You can wear this! You'll look great in this!!

She starts to take FRANKIE*'s jumper off her.* FRANKIE *finishes the job herself, turning away a fraction. She is in her bra or a strap top. She has a nicotine patch on her arm.*

What's this?

FRANKIE. My arm.

SARAH. You smoke?

FRANKIE. Not any more.

I thought we were going dancing.

SARAH. We are. We are! Do people still go to Infernos?

*

In the club. It is bright and loud. They dance together and alone. FRANKIE *is hesitant until she is not. They are free and it is glorious.*

*

SARAH*'s house.* SARAH *is bleeding from the nose/mouth.* FRANKIE *is trying to tend to her face.* SARAH *won't let her do it properly, if at all.*

FRANKIE. Why did you tell her who you were? Are?

SARAH. She recognised me.

FRANKIE. How? You aren't dressed like, you look completely different.

SARAH. She said, I know you from somewhere. She kept
saying it. She wouldn't shut up. I was just trying to wash my
hands. 'I know you.' 'Do we work together?' 'Are you from
Nottingham?' 'Are you Fiona so-and-so's sister?' 'I swear
down I know you.'

So I told her.

FRANKIE. Why would you do that?

SARAH. She called me an evil bitch. And then she punched me.
The first one didn't – so she did it again and again and then the
attendant started shouting and these girls grabbed her –

FRANKIE. Let me sort your face out.

SARAH. It's fine.

FRANKIE. You're bleeding. Here –

SARAH *bats her away.*

For god's sake. You shouldn't have told her, Sarah. We could
have left. We shouldn't have gone. I said we shouldn't go.

SARAH. It was fun before that though, wasn't it?

FRANKIE. I think I'm going to be sick.

SARAH. Shh, shh. Okay. Just.

SARAH *readies* FRANKIE *to be sick. Holds her hair back if
needs be, rubs her back.* FRANKIE *retches. Nothing comes.*

They collapse. Still tipsy.

You shouldn't have smoked. Give me the fags. And the lighter.

FRANKIE. The lighter –

SARAH. What?

FRANKIE. It's sentimental.

SARAH. Sentimental?

FRANKIE. Mr Taylor.

SARAH. He gave you a lighter?

FRANKIE. Yeah.

SARAH. Then you're definitely handing it over. Fucking hell. Fucking hell.

FRANKIE *hands them over.*

FRANKIE. Can I ask you something? Why did you –

SARAH. I'm drunk! She wouldn't shut up and I just wanted to shock her –

FRANKIE. No. No. The other day. With the talc. You tasted it.

SARAH. That was weeks ago. It was talc.

FRANKIE. We didn't know that.

SARAH. What else could it have been?

FRANKIE. We both thought it was something – dangerous.

SARAH. I thought it was talc.

FRANKIE. You didn't think it was talc. You stopped. You froze. You thought what I thought.

SARAH. Which was what?

FRANKIE. That it was anthrax! That's what it was meant to look like. Like anthrax.

SARAH. Tad dramatic, Frankie. We're not in 2001.

FRANKIE. They sent it to look like anthrax.

SARAH. To look like but it wasn't!

FRANKIE. It could have been!

SARAH. But it wasn't.

FRANKIE. That's not the fucking point!

You couldn't be sure. What are you doing? The girl tonight. Putting your hair up. Going all those places.

SARAH. Frankie.

FRANKIE. That girl punched you. The things people write in the letters, on Twitter –

SARAH. It was talcum powder. I'm okay. You're okay. Can we
drop –

FRANKIE. Do you want to kill yourself?

#

SARAH. Why would I want that?

FRANKIE. Okay. Fine.

SARAH. Frankie.

I won't lick any more talcum powder if you decide what
you're going to do about the fact you're pregnant.

#

FRANKIE. What.

SARAH. You're constantly running to the loo, you've given up
smoking, you're getting fat and I can smell the vomit on
your breath most days.

I thought you might be bulimic.

FRANKIE. I'm not bulimic.

SARAH. Evidently.

FRANKIE. Why did you let me drink?

SARAH. Are you going to be sick?

FRANKIE. No.

SARAH. Do you want to be sick?

FRANKIE. Yes.

SARAH. Here.

She puts her fingers down FRANKIE*'s throat. Helps her
to retch.*

FRANKIE. I don't like going outside with you. It ruins
everything.

8.

SARAH's flat. Two days later. A teddy with a telescope.
A newspaper.

FRANKIE. It's a massive deal.

SARAH. It's on what? Page nine?

FRANKIE. It's all over the internet. There's no page nine on the
internet. They're furious.

SARAH. I want to tell you about the Observatory. I was stood
on this line and had one foot / in the Eastern Hemisphere
[and one foot in the Western Hemisphere].

FRANKIE. Can you just – for once, Sarah?

Did you see him?

SARAH. Who?

FRANKIE. The photographer.

SARAH. I was Dancing, Frankie. You were Dancing.

FRANKIE. You're looking right at the camera.

SARAH. I'm already getting death threats.

FRANKIE. Yeah. *You're* already getting death threats.

SARAH. Oh, this is about you?

FRANKIE. They're making us out to be some kind of cabal.

SARAH. I think a cabal has more than two people, surely?
We'd need another couple of murderesses and their pregnant,
lesbian lovers for it to be a cabal.

Frankie? I'm being quite hilarious and you're giving me
nothing.

FRANKIE. What if someone realises it's me.

SARAH. You can barely see your face.

FRANKIE. My mum –

SARAH. Your mum reads the *Express*?

FRANKIE. Not everyone reads the *Sunday* fucking *Times*.

SARAH. More's the pity.

FRANKIE. Sarah, it's like we're happy she's dead. Like we
bonded over her being dead. Like we're celebrating. Like
we're heartless.

SARAH. Do you think I'm happy?

FRANKIE. Of course not. Of course not.

SARAH. Do you think one second goes by when I wouldn't rip
open every vein in my body, every vein in your body to get
her back.

#

FRANKIE. They are so angry at you. Between the interview
and now this. This guy on Twitter said if he found the black
bitch that was with you, he'd lynch her. There's a lot of stuff
like that.

It frightens me.

SARAH. I understand. Of course you're scared. I'm scared.

FRANKIE. You don't seem scared, you seem –

SARAH. What?

FRANKIE. Thrilled.

SARAH. What do you want me to do, Frankie?

FRANKIE. My flatmates talked about you, at pre-drinks like
how they'd talk about *Love Island*. Luke, the Rugby guy, said
they should sew up your womb with a rusty needle. I got
really angry. I flipped. And they were like why do you love her
so much, why do you care?

They're going to realise it's me and I can't have that
conversation. I can't. I don't want to go back there.

SARAH. Stay here.

FRANKIE. I can't.

SARAH. Why?

FRANKIE. Are you [sure]?

SARAH. Yes.

FRANKIE. I can sleep on the sofa.

SARAH. Don't be ridiculous. There's a room. Bring Copernicus.

>FRANKIE *picks up the teddy with the telescope.*

>I'm very sorry they're being. That it's a racial thing.

FRANKIE. It's always been a racial thing. You think a black mum would have been let off with no charges?

SARAH. Come on.

*

They are in Rosie's room. The crib.

FRANKIE. I can sleep on the sofa. This is.

SARAH. No, it's okay.

>SARAH *begins to take apart the crib.*

FRANKIE. We can push it to the side.

SARAH. I've got to do it at some point.

>He's trying to sell the house unseen. He'll get a hundred grand less but he can't bear the thought of me here. So.

>SARAH *continues to take apart the crib.* FRANKIE *sits down too and begins to help.*

>*They don't speak except murmured instructions on how to dismantle it.*

>*It takes some time. It is an endeavour.*

>*Eventually, they are done. They sit amongst the ruins.*

>FRANKIE *begins to cry.* SARAH *holds her feet.*

FRANKIE. Can you stop going to all these places. Just while it dies down again. Please? I can't – if something happened to you.

SARAH. I don't think [anything is going to happen to me].

FRANKIE. Please, Sarah.

SARAH. I promise.

How long have you known you're pregnant?

FRANKIE. The day before I came here. The first time. When I painted your nails.

SARAH. How far gone are you?

FRANKIE. Um. Sixteen weeks.

#

You haven't asked me what I'm going to do.

SARAH. We both know what you're going to do.

FRANKIE. I have thought about it. Keeping it. This one girl, Shauna Akers, she was like white-girl loud, you knew she wasn't going to do much with her life. We sat next to each other in RE until she got pregnant in Year 10. Everyone said it was the Making of Her. The first time she took herself, her life seriously. Her baby was the Making of Her. She did some kind of midwifery thing. She posts a lot about the miracle of birth on Facebook.

And I wondered. Wonder. If maybe, maybe it would be the Making of Me. I'm not necessarily doing so great. Obviously. At school, I was winning poetry competitions and getting A-stars and being a person. But here. I don't go in. I don't get up. I do things I shouldn't. I don't. I don't even brush my teeth some days. Some weeks. I can't look after myself.

Did I tell you I got two A-stars and an A for A level? I know I've got to brush my teeth and go to my lectures but part of me just goes – (*Shrugs.*) just – (*Shrugs again.*) So I stay in bed. And my teeth hurt and yellow and I don't go out and I don't call my mum and I ignore Lucy knocking on my door and I feel disgusting. But I am disgusting so at least the outside – [matches the inside].

The only time I really leave is to come here. To see you.

I thought if maybe I had someone who I had to. You know. Teach to about the tooth fairy.

I know. Really. I know a baby isn't a cure for – anything. But I just think about it. Thought about it.

I thought too that maybe there was another choice. I could still –

SARAH. What?

FRANKIE *considers her. Goes to say something. Changes her mind.*

FRANKIE. I booked one. Next Thursday at eleven. It's in Richmond. The local clinic is closed for refurbishment. Which I thought was – you don't think about clinics being closed for refurbishment. What are they doing, getting hardwood floors?

SARAH. I'll take you.

FRANKIE. It's fine. I'll get the train there and I was going to get an Uber back.

SARAH. Don't be ridiculous.

FRANKIE. You don't, you don't have to do that.

SARAH. I know.

You can say it you know. Abortion. You haven't even said the word.

FRANKIE. I know.

She doesn't say it.

Do you hate me?

SARAH. Not at all.

I'm fine, Frankie.

FRANKIE. I don't understand how you can be.

SARAH. I'm okay.

FRANKIE. You don't talk about Rosie.

SARAH. Maybe that's why I'm okay.

FRANKIE. If you wanted to – to talk about her. It might make you feel –

SARAH. I feel fine.

FRANKIE. Do you ever think about having another one?

SARAH. I think it would be the unmaking of me.

FRANKIE. But but if there was a way –

FRANKIE takes SARAH's hand and places it on her belly. She is testing.

SARAH looks searchingly at FRANKIE.

An offer.

SARAH keeps her hand on FRANKIE's stomach. Then she is on her knees with her head against FRANKIE's stomach. She stays there for such a long time.

She stands up. There might for a moment be the feeling that she might slap FRANKIE.

She doesn't.

SARAH. I think you should leave.

FRANKIE. You said [I could stay].

SARAH. No one is going to recognise you. Nothing is going to happen to you. No one cares about you. You're nothing to do with this.

FRANKIE leaves.

9.

Inside SARAH*'s car. Outside the clinic.*

FRANKIE. Thank you for coming to get me. I was just about to
   order an Uber, I could have –

SARAH. How do you feel?

FRANKIE. Sore. Tired.

   #

   Are these seats heated?

SARAH. Yes.

FRANKIE. Of course, you have heated seats.

   #

   Sarah, the other day –

SARAH. Do you want the radio on?

FRANKIE. Okay. That would be, yeah. I might fall asleep.

SARAH. That's fine. Oh. It's not working.

   It's not. It won't turn on.

FRANKIE. It doesn't matter.

   #

   SARAH *sings under her breath. Something that sounds
   a little like a lullaby but isn't. Faltering. For a while.*
   FRANKIE *is falling asleep.*

   Is this, is this the same car?

SARAH. Yes.

   I replaced the window.

   A moment.

                              *

Rosie's room. FRANKIE *is curled up.*

SARAH. Do you want some water?

FRANKIE. No.

SARAH. Wine?

FRANKIE. No.

SARAH. You want me to go?

FRANKIE. No.

>SARAH *touches* FRANKIE *tentatively.*

>I wish I could tell my mum [everything].

>SARAH *is overcome. She moves closer to* FRANKIE.
>*Holds her properly.* FRANKIE *begins to fall asleep in*
>SARAH*'s arms.*

10.

SARAH*'s flat. The following morning.*

SARAH *puts her hair up with great specificity. She puts on the
blue coat. She leaves.*

*

FRANKIE *wakes up. Confused to be alone. Still slightly sore.
Remembering yesterday. Agitated. She doesn't know what to do
with herself.*

*

She tidies the bears.

*

She looks at her phone.

*

*She finds some unopened letters. Begins to open them. One or
two and then. She opens another and is shocked, angry, hurt.*

*

She is going to leave.

SARAH *returns.*

SARAH. You're meant to be resting.

FRANKIE. Where have you been?

SARAH. Out.

FRANKIE. To where exactly?

> SARAH *produces a bear wearing a deerstalker, with a pipe and magnifying glass.* FRANKIE *does not take it.*

SARAH. Come on. Elementary, my dear Miss Frankie... It's Sherlock Holmes. Did you even know there's a Sherlock Holmes Museum? Next to Baker Street!

It was fifteen pounds entry. Full of foreign teenagers who had no idea who I was – salivating over that actor. And I realised I don't really care for detective stories.

Frankie?

FRANKIE. I asked you not to do this.

SARAH. I know you're tired but I could really / do without the third degree.

FRANKIE. You got a letter.

SARAH. Right. If it's about the house, I was going to tell you –

FRANKIE. Tell me what?

SARAH. What? He sold it. He lost a lot on it; the graffiti, the lack of viewings, survey, the general pervading miasma of misery. But he's sold it.

FRANKIE. Sarah! Where are you going to live?

SARAH. That doesn't matter.

Maybe I'll burn it down.

That's not about the house?

FRANKIE. It's from your mum.

SARAH. Oh.

FRANKIE. I thought she was dead?

SARAH. You assumed she was dead. I'm not that old.

FRANKIE. You said – you always said you have no one.

SARAH. I don't know how I feel about you opening my post.

FRANKIE. You said – always – that everyone had left you.
It says you kicked her out, that she's happy to give you space
but her and your dad are worried about you and miss you and
love you and they want you to forgive yourself. She talks
about him – Steven – him selling the house isn't some
terrible conspiracy. He's just this hurt man who loves you
and wants you to be / outside of this.

SARAH. You read one letter and know you know the inner
workings of my family? You should have the deerstalker,
Frankie. A proper detective.

FRANKIE. I can't do this.

SARAH. Can't do what.

FRANKIE. This.

SARAH. I'm going to need another noun, Frankie.

FRANKIE. Why are you still driving that car?

SARAH. It didn't make financial sense to get a new one. It still
doesn't. Maybe next year once I get my portion of the / sale.

FRANKIE. How much did it cost to replace the window and get
my blood cleaned?

SARAH. I don't know.

FRANKIE. If you were worried about money, you would know.
The only people who don't know how much things cost are
people who don't have to worry about money.

SARAH. This isn't the price of milk –

FRANKIE. She died in there. It's like her fucking tomb and you
kept it and you drive it and you picked me up and made me
sit in there!

SARAH. I'm sorry for picking you up from your abortion, Frankie, what do you want me to say?

FRANKIE. I think this is over.

SARAH. What is THIS?

FRANKIE. This – you and me – this.

SARAH. Are you *dumping* me?!

FRANKIE. I am so sick of watching you pretend to be okay all the while –

SARAH. All the while What?

FRANKIE. Walking around in that coat, telling that girl who you are, the stunts in the press. Everything you've done, everything you're doing.

SARAH. I'm not going to beg for anyone's forgiveness.

FRANKIE. You're begging for someone to throw acid in your face, aren't you?

#

SARAH. What should I be doing? Staying in bed for weeks and asking men from craigslist to fuck me whilst I cry?

FRANKIE. That is not what this is / about.

SARAH. You are sad, Frankie and you've been sad for a long, long time. Then one day you find a dead baby and you get to feel like some brave, brave girl. Part of some big tragedy. Something terrible finally happened to Frankie so it's okay that she wants to kill herself.

But that is my. It is my pain. And it's not contagious and it's not healing and it's not magic, it's nothing and it's mine.

FRANKIE. That's not –

SARAH. If you want a reason to kill yourself, find something else, Frankie. I'm not your excuse.

FRANKIE. And I'm not your replacement daughter.

That hits.

SARAH. It's not my fault your mother has no idea how to love you.

FRANKIE. You don't have to do this. None of this has to be like this.

SARAH. Get out. GET OUT.

FRANKIE exits.

SARAH takes in everything around her. The empty house. The bears.

*

She reads the letter from her mother, rips it up.

*

She picks up the pieces of the cot tries to put them together.

*

She readjusts her hair. The coat.

She takes out the letter from Scene Four. She reads it again. She rings the number.

Hello? Is this Adam? My name is Sarah. Sarah Hargreave. You wrote me a letter.

Hello? Adam? Hello?

Another disappointment.

*

She gets out a teddy we haven't seen before. A classic one. The kind you'd give to a newborn, soft. It has been loved. She holds it.

*

SARAH *takes a breath.*

*

She finds the graffiti-removal liquid.

She pours the liquid around the house, around the stage. Dousing everything.

She takes out FRANKIE*'s lighter.*

She holds it ready. She prepares herself. It was always, always going to end like this.

11.

FRANKIE*'s university. A seminar room.*

A bright-white light is projected, as though she is using slides. Nothing appears on the slides.

FRANKIE. In the Torah, these are called Arei Miklat. The Book of Numbers records God's command to Moses to pick six cities – Numbers 35: 11 'then you shall appoint cities to be cities of refuge for you, that the manslayer who kills any person accidentally may flee there.' God goes on to delineate between what modern-day parlance would see as the difference between murder and manslaughter. Those that commit manslaughter, those that accidentally kill are to be welcomed into the Refuge cities for protection and to be given space for atonement. It is Joshua who finally establishes these Refuge cities, choosing Kedesh, Shechem, Kirjath Arba, Golan, Ramoth and Bezer. I'll stay on this slide so you can get those spellings down. Or I can email them around after. Okay? Diverting to the Talmud, according to Rabbinical footnotes from the thirteenth century, the roads which led to the cities of Refuge were to be wider than regular roads and well signposted – so that anyone who accidentally killed someone could be protected by God without delay. A place of protection and atonement. A sanctuary.

An interesting thought when we begin to move towards the New Testament and take on Paul's notions of…

12.

A kind of, not quite hospital room. Clean and white.

FRANKIE *enters – holding a bagful of takeaway containers.*

FRANKIE. Have you eaten?

SARAH. Frankie. You came.

What's this?

FRANKIE. What does it look like?

SARAH. I don't know

FRANKIE. It's a taste-test. Every lamb curry with yogurt in the greater Fulham area.

Last supper and all.

SARAH. They're cold.

FRANKIE. Yeah, I had to get them all the way here then past the staff. Do you want to ask Nurse Ratched for a microwave?

#

SARAH. It's always better the next day, anyway.

SARAH *tastes them. One by one. A ritual.*

After the first few it kind of –

FRANKIE. All tastes the same?

They laugh. She continues.

SARAH. It's this one. It's this one.

FRANKIE *takes the bag it was taken from, there's a menu stuck to the side.*

FRANKIE. It's from Miraj takeaway, Putney.

SARAH. Oh.

FRANKIE. It's the, I can't pronounce it Raja–

SARAH. Rajasthani lamb. You found it.

FRANKIE. Yeah. So you can, you can order it now.

I brought this too. I figure you might not have had time to find the gift shop.

It's the old teddy.

\#

SARAH. I didn't know psych wards had gift shops.

FRANKIE *is a bit overcome*.

Hey, it's fine.

FRANKIE. I got a first on my presentation. So I passed the year.

SARAH. That's amazing! Frankie, that's. I'm so proud of you.

Are you still going to take some time out – what do they call it?

FRANKIE. 'Interrupting my studies'? Yeah. I'm going to go home-home for a bit.

SARAH. Have you told your mum yet?

FRANKIE. Not yet.

If I wasn't going back home for a bit. If I stayed, stayed at uni, stayed in London, you'd still think that we have to stop seeing each other wouldn't you?

SARAH. It's good that you're going home. You need your mum. What I said. It wasn't true. I was angry.

FRANKIE. It's okay... I wouldn't know how to love me either.

SARAH. Frankie, no. It's remarkably easy [to love you].

It's like this for a lot of people. You know, your early twenties. Sorry, I'm not. I know part of it is being unwell. Depressed. Just that. The other bit. This feeling. This lost feeling that will go one day.

FRANKIE. You seem lost, still.

SARAH. I can't go home to my mum.

FRANKIE. Only, you can.

You could call me?

SARAH. Frankie.

FRANKIE. Facebook? Of course not, that's. I'll write you a letter.

SARAH. Minus the anthrax?

FRANKIE. If I come back to finish my degree –

SARAH. When you come back.

FRANKIE. Could we?

SARAH. Yeah, maybe.

She means no – and they both know it.

FRANKIE. Yeah. Okay. What are you going to do, now?

SARAH. I'll need to find somewhere to live, I suppose. Find the new best Rajathstani lamb. Then I thought I might go away.

FRANKIE. Where?

SARAH. Maybe America. I might go find that support group. I could update their web design.

FRANKIE. You're not going to do that.

SARAH. Probably not.

FRANKIE. Nobody would know who you are out there.

SARAH. Yes, thought it might be a good thing.

FRANKIE. Yeah.

There's something I want to say and I don't know how to so I'm just going to. If Rosie had grown up and had shitty boyfriends or hated university or been sad, you would have been –

SARAH. Frankie –

FRANKIE. No, you would have been everything she needed.

SARAH. You coming back when you did and how you got me safe and well, got me here, I suppose. You were very brave, Frankie and you saved me.

FRANKIE. No you – you [saved me].

SARAH. I know.

FRANKIE. Good. I was going to give you this back but I guess?

SARAH. I can give it to the new people. It's a family. They could probably do with spares.

FRANKIE. Yeah.

FRANKIE hands SARAH the key. Their hands meet and join, they're saying goodbye. Everything they say next is entirely inadequate but they say it anyway.

SARAH. *Call* your mum. And look after yourself. Brush your teeth and stay off craigslist and get well and.

FRANKIE. Yeah. Yeah. Let me um let me know how Tinder goes.

They are in their own spaces, simultaneously. Unaware of each other but impossibly connected.

SARAH eats from the right curry. She is comforted. It is enough. She holds the bear.

FRANKIE goes around, picking up all the bears. She puts them in a bin liner. Except the lemur. She holds it in her arms and dials.

Hi, Mum. Yeah, yeah, no I'm probably not really okay.

End.

End note

The phenomenon described in this play is real, terrible and
entirely not the fault of the parents. For more information,
I would point readers to kidsandcars.org and Gene Weingarten's
Washington Post article 'Fatal Distraction' which is a very hard
read but explains the science and humanity behind the headlines.

A Nick Hern Book

soft animals first published as a paperback original in Great Britain in 2019 by Nick Hern Books Limited, The Glasshouse, 49a Goldhawk Road, London W12 8QP, in association with Soho Theatre, London

Cover image by Jonathan Birch Photography

Designed and typeset by Nick Hern Books, London
Printed in the UK by Mimeo Ltd, Huntingdon, Cambridgeshire PE29 6XX

A CIP catalogue record for this book is available from the British Library

ISBN   978 1 84842 843 0